BEAUTY

ManChild!

Innocence trapped in a vile body,
Tainted by the pleasures of the flesh.
In the servitude of canal desires, you
have devoted yourself,
Oh! ManChild how ignorant you are?
To believe that you have grown up
for old you have grown
but the child in you still lives.
Nurtured by man's eyes you speak,
Speak only the words that entice the ear.
In perpetual arguments and fights,
your soul rejoices
giving glory to your masculinity
and shielding your inner fear.

THE STAR

I have wandered from afar
in the dark gloomy night,
but as I look
in the clear blue sky
there you lay.
The star

the star that guides a lost soul.

As I staggered through the valley
with fear invading my heart
leaving me to wonder
could this be the end?

But still, you lay steadily
in the clear blue sky
You ! a star that guides a lost soul.
Like the constant whisper of the summer breeze,
your presence acts as a reminder
that I'll never be alone.

REKINDLE

I feel the flame in my soul slowly fading
could it be the predicaments
and impediments of this lonely world
that seek to wipe out the fire in my soul?
I search for the fire
that used to fuel my desire,
But all I find are the ashes of pain.
Rekindle rekindle
rekindle the fierce burning flame in my heart.
My soul wanders in the world of dreams
in a quest to reinvent the soldier in me
as my knees are weakened

by the dire events of this world
crippling the desire to move forward.
But like the smile of young sunshine
hope will rise again
To rekindle the flame of fame,
and restore me to my former glory.

QUEEN OF HEARTS

As she walks down slowly through the pavement
her warm, cozy and tender smile lures men
to her path.
Her hour-glass body curves
them into young children,
Like young children sulking
over their mother's breast
their eyes sulk at her beauty with wonder.
While other women utter
silently behind closed doors
for her beauty makes all women vulnerable.

SOLDIER LOVE

Bombarded by an estranged feeling
my heart turned to an ocean of carnal desires.
My heart wonders about this estranged feeling
could it be love?
Love turns wise men into zombies of affection.
I've longed for such a feeling
that acts as a catalyst of
self-denial and selflessness
Love is a warrior that conquers
the perils of this world of solitude.

Gunned down by her melodious words
I bleed only blood of fleshly pleasures.
For her beauty is like that of a warrior
that merges victorious in all battles.
A victim of canal desires
and pure lust I've become,
for her beauty destroys my mechanical defenses
I have fallen prey to her lustful ways.

THE GRIEVING ORPHAN

She wandered the earth like a lost sheep
searching for comfort in this solitary world,
hopping and hoping for a glimpse of love.
Her heart was bombarded with sadness,
she sought comfort in a strange man's arms
Her walls of defense came
crashing down for the strange man

had gained victory over her.

Grief has turned her into a menace,
for she seeks comfort in thorny bushes.
Wounded by life she continues,
whilst her heart silently explodes with pain,
the pain of the grieving orphan
that knows temporal love of a man's body warmth.
What she knows not is that
beyond her meek mighty pain
lies the happiness she seeks.

SUDDEN DEATH

A terrifying sound was heard
as she slowly slipped downhill
The angel of death had robbed her of her existence.
Her sickness became a mystery
not known even to the wisest of men.
The whole world was left in shock,
for they knew not of the
silent thunder tormenting her heart.
A delicate flower with thorns,
the feeble vigorous being suffering
from a dire disease not known to men.

Her beauty was that of the
morning sun in a harsh winter,
Her melodious voice was like

that of the sound of the birds.
The battle continues
as her soul wafts in the air,
a futile attempt to free herself.
Like an infant robbed of its childhood
the world is left with a void
that makes them mourn helplessly
leaving them to wonder did she have to DIE.

SUICIDE NOTE

Buried under the barricades of my thought
Covered it with a smile,
that the world was soon to endorse.
A deep smile screaming for help
Till the only sound, I heard was that of my own,
A battle with my demons that holds a futile end.

PRISONER!

A wound caused by self-mortification
a soul forced to succumb to inevitable pain.
Your heart mourns with great agony
for it is a prisoner of the mind.

Oh! how you have fallen prey
to hedonistic desires.
A hailstorm resides in your mind
for you know only the shivering warmth of winter.

How long shall you be a prisoner of
your thoughts?
Or the destroyer of your fate.
For you have allowed peril
to triumph over your mind
and death to be the messiah of your life.

SAVIOUR

Oh, glorious waters how precious you are
a fortress of the sea animals
and the birds of the air
Dreams are quenched with your mighty drops
and the land replenishes in your honor.
You give strength to the weak
with your everlasting shine,
shine that lures voyagers
to confide in your sacred walls.
Awe ! men of little gratitude
how you have prickled the skin of the waters.
Glorious waters
have turned into an ocean of blood
caused by nature's narcissism.

Fortress turned to ruins
and a place of solitude
by its inhabitants
care 'st not that you have tainted its innocence?

THE HEARTBREAK

The rate of my heart is slowly deteriorating
Numb and still I lay,
for my heart has lost its purpose.
For a moment everything seems still,
the world around me is fading.
what used to be our home is now a house of ruins
my skin slowly turns pale,
my words escape me
the plants around me wither regarding my loss.

Looking through space I see
yesterday when we sang jolly songs
of unending happiness
rapped in fluffy bags of love.
Suddenly a black owl passes by
leaving me to immerse myself in melancholy,
Slowly I embrace my loss
finding strength in discomfort
for the door of love has been unlocked.

THE LONE WOLF

A wild feline that survives
by licking its wounds
predictor to all animals
but prey to its instinct.
Walking past the woods the flies chant,
chants of the glory of your island self.
In servitude, the trees
wave making melodious sounds
while you watch the grass beneath you bow down
in its exhausted self
For their grey hairs
mark the end of your reign.

SILENT SCREAM

A loud noise reoccurs in my mind,
silent screams that threaten my being.
In this holocaust, I find no comfort or peace
Thoughts torment, my soul, as I slowly
sail through this stormy path.
From the ashes, a revolution has risen
causing the death of my innocent soul,
leaving my heart to wonder
how loud can this silent scream be?

SISTER

At the helm of the sunset, we fought
to strengthen the depth of our bond.
In your presence I rejoice and
mourn your absence
for distance is a slow but deadly poison.
Your presence is toxic to my being
causing me to slowly
suffocate in your rude but kind self.
Through the persistent fight,
you have proved your undying love for me
your words penetrate my heart as a two-sided world
my heart bleeds with unending love for you.
My tears are but a reflection of your pain
your love is like cloudberries
for it is the source of my happiness
and eventually the cause of my death.

SAVIOUR COMPLEX

Consumed by guilt you serve
with a white heart tainted

with a dark soul while your
consciousness slowly devours you.
Your house has become a fortress for strays
your wealth a fountain for the poor,
The bed that you lay in is an ocean of tears
for you know grace has forsaken you,
Her attempts to save you
from yourself have been futile.
In anger, she has cursed your soul
to be an invisible servant.
From dawn till dusk you will serve
your efforts will become
light but you shall never be known.
Let the tornado in your mind create chaos
till your heart bleeds for redemption.
In serving the meek you will
devote your life while they bloom
like autumn roses you will swell and wither.

LOST

Amidst all the creatures your nature
has turned you into a rebel.
Humorous sounds they sang till you
opened your mouth to roar thunder.
A lost soul you are
for you know not the righteous path.

Your presence is like a harsh breeze

in summer afternoon
summer afternoon. Your beauty succumbs to your
thorny behavior.
A lost soul you are
for you know not peace.

Wandering in the faces of the earth
while the trees stare in despair
for they know they have
lost sight of your path.
A lost soul you are for
you know only a desolate path.

ON THE 13TH OF NOVEMBER

rebuked me for mourning
my heart exploded with thunderous pain
The news of your death came as a surprise
yet I wondered
if is it possible to be heartbroken
over a man who caused your first heartbreak?
To be able to feel pain for the arbiter of your pain,
my mind became overwhelmed.
Gone is the man who fathered
pain and resentment, leaving the world
to wail and murmur in sorrow.
Yesterday you sat in your chair
of glory and I felt belittled.
Today the world calls out to me to mourn,

my tears escape me.
And as I walk the earth
with my head held high
I remember your words
' Let it hurt till it hurts no more
but never let the world know your pain'.

THREE ANGELS

Gloriously clothed with a purple robe
you clot the vicious globe
stripping it out of its guilty pleasures.
Clouded by their myopic views
they cry out for these so-called
treasures causing the ocean in their eyes
to tear for the only way you can
save them is by instilling fear.

In the dark, they delight
for they are the cabinet
that rules the devil's throne
their err's are but shadows
that disappear at dawn
for in the morning,
they are made judges of immorality
till the sun shies away
again and monsters they become.

Lofting in the air you command

the weak to rise and in the face
of the wicked, you have roared
leaving the soil underneath
to crumble for the thunder
in your voice has caused
a shift to its core.

Your melodious voices give a sense of comfort
to the bruised hearts
of the widows and orphans.
For in your lap the weary harbor
yearning for nothing for
they have found peace at last.

A WOMAN'S LAMENT

Through the wound of pain I breath
for I have become like a caged bird,
looking through a broken window I
what could have been my tomorrow?
Yesterday in battle
I fought with a pen and paper
today they are the reason for my execution.

Living in the torment of Hitler's rule
I cover myself with a veil of sorrow.
Articulating my voice in the silence,
because a woman's opinion has become taboo.
Early this morning a detonator

was heard the birds slowly retreated and hid
leaving the sky to clothe
themselves with sackcloth.

Like a thief at night hope slowly creeps in
ripping the fear instilled by the iron rod,
Mother nature has rebelled
against these gruesome acts causing
the victims to look up at the sky
for a silver lining has blossomed
due to the tears that have fertilized the soil.
Songs of victory pervade the sky
as the birds mock and rebuke such vicious acts.

THE MORNING WHISPER

Like the blackbird, I wake up
to be caressed by
gentle fingers of the sun.
While the morning breeze whispers
news of delight into my ears.
I hear the whisper again,
my heart melts
for nature has ruled in my favor.

THE UNWELCOMED VISITOR

You creep at night to strip
us of a chance at happiness,
in the flow of our tears, you delight
for you are hungry for souls.
Your cousin's destruction and depression
passed by last night,
with chaos and grief they left.
The soothsayer informed us of
your dreadful smile that was cast upon us,
how do we smile back when pain invades our minds?
With constant joy,
you have taken our beloved
and made our hearts wail for we know
as time passes so shall you visit again.

FORBIDDEN LOVE

As my eyes set sight on you, my soul yearns
for that which may never be.
Loving you from afar has made my
heart content.
Your happiness is like a ray of sunshine
that tickles the yoke of my heart
My happiness resides in yours
for when tears drop from your eyes
my heart drowns in sorrow.
A connection far greater than

this world can ever comprehend,
a feeling so pure the heart
cannot begin to embrace
but still can never be!
For when our hearts combine
so shall the world perish?

THE VIRUS

In despair and isolation, we breathe,
as we watch our fellow friends and family
departing to the land of the dead.
Like autumn leaves turning pale we silently watch
the memories we once had faded away
for you have made us an iland.

Oh! how unforgiving you are
for you have cursed us
to never see our beloved again.
Funeral songs have become a norm,
our eyes are like a dried-up fountain.
You are an invisible enemy
whose attack is fatal and without warning.

Days pass and so does the hope to be set free,
for you have made us prisoners in our own homes.
As we stagger through life
we stare through the window of time
reminiscing of times we took for granted.

Slowly we grow to envy
the animals and rebuke you
for your wrath holds no bond.

THE LAMENT OF A MAN

I am but just a man
a man of virtue, a man of honor.
When I raise my hand to a woman
it is but to comfort and greet.
I have dedicated my life
to uplifting my female companion
but behind closed doors, I weep and wail invisible tears.

I am but just a man
a man with a kind and loving heart.
For I have used my masculinity to shield
and protect my female companion
but blade and nail bruise my skin.

I am but just a man
a man of strength, a man of skill.
I comfort the weary and help the needy
but I am not of any help to myself.
For the tears of a man are regarded as a weakness
and so I shall suffer in silence
till my heart breaks and I am laid to rest.

KIND HEART

No pain is greater than having a kind heart
nor joy greater than being a kind man.
For soon everyone around you shall depart
and in solitude, you will remain in motion.
Blessed you are to be in servitude
to everyone in need for when their hopeless souls
stare into your eyes they believe,
it is then that you realize how much you have
achieved.

CHILDHOOD DREAMS

Once upon a time, I cared not,
I threw caution to the wind and rode the waves.
In small things, I found delight,
and in big ones a reason to go further.
But today my heart is weakened by kindness
and my will, crippled by opinions.
Oh! how much I would give
to return to my childhood self
and calm the vortex in my heart.
For as the sun sets I'll take heed and fly

At least my strength eroded by aging
I shall reclaim my childhood spirit.

AFRICAN PRIDE

Africa my Africa the land of pride
the land of culture.
As I stretch my ears to the north
I hear drums giving thanks to the ancestor.
When I turn my eyes to the south
I see the smoke of incest burning.
Pure African pride and culture.

Africa my Africa a land that replenishes
due to our forefather's blood.
Tunning their heart to the soil
their sweat fertilized the soil.
Today we sing and dance for they set us free.

BROTHER

Dear brother, you despise me
not because I am evil
but because I represent what you wanted to be.

You find comfort in my torment
and joy in my sadness.
I travel through mountains and rivers
in search of comfort and closure
for the war between us tears my soul.

PEACE AND WAR

When lightning strikes
the wise take heed and hide
for they are in sink with nature.
Nurturing their talents
they know the calming sounds of thunder
and the relieving touch of rain.
For when the clouds roar
they know the soil has sent out an invitation.
Man and nature sing harmonious sounds
while the ants cultivate the land beneath
so shall man listen
for the final stroke of thunder?

Awe! man of little gratitude
for you have plucked out nature's hairs
and burned her clothes,
you have defied nature's law.
As the moon bleeds the clouds go into mourning
for the earth has been stripped naked.
The earth retreats in shame,

leaving the sun to torment man till
the clouds strike lightning again to seal man's fate.

ANGEL

A sweetly scented soul thou art
dressed with a consistent smile that comforts.
Thou beauty succumbs a garden full of roses.
The whole world is left to murmur at thou presence
as your garden overflows with purple lilies.
Impeccable and without flaws thou art
like an ocean that overflows,
with one thought in mind
will I ever go dry?

SORROWFUL DAWN

A distant sound pervades my ear
my heart battles with my chest in an attempt to escape,
for a moment it stops beating.
As I look through the window,
dawn! it is then that I know death has passed by.
Just as the pain seizes to disappear

you visit again to remind us of the pain you cause.
The death you never let us forget,
for in the darkest of dawn,
you show your unremorseful face.
As we sleep our hearts shut down
in an attempt to hide from your face
because you never let us forget the pain.

A FATHER'S DYING WISH

Promise me you never change
promise me that you will not
allow the predicaments of this world to corrupt you.
Promise me that you will keep your
head held high at all times,
that you will walk past the storm
and never lose your smile.
Promise me that the glittering world
will not corrupt your morality and principles.
Promise me my child that you will not
allow grief to triumph in your heart.
Swear to never let the comfort of this world
rip the concept of hard work from your mind.
Take pride in the blood of your roots
for if you know where you come from
the path to your destination shall not forsake you.

THE FEATHERLESS EAGLE

I gaze toward the sky,
and all I see are locked doors.
I search for a path but thorns fill my way,
I have no will to go on.
Being in crowds makes me feel lonely hence
I resort to isolation.
Anxiety befriends my soul,
swearing to never leave me alone.
A friend, at last, that will never leave.
I rise and set for the sky but the forces
of life weigh heavy on my shoulders.
I retreat in silence,
covering my face with a veil of
shame, I swear never to fly again.
My vision is obscured by the clotting veins
in my eyes .
I am an enemy to myself,
sinking my claws through my skin
I curve a wound on my back
to remind me never to fly again.

LOVE AND HATRADE

Who knows pain and grief more than one who loves
or who knows isolation than one who hates?
For love teaches one how to tolerate pain
and hate forces one to face their defects.
For when love and hate co-exist the world
lives in perfect harmony.

DEADLY SILENCE

I've often wondered why the thunder roars
but causes no damage,
yet lightning is the silent killer.
Why the water so still has the power to take a life
and a flame so small can cause great chaos.
Why the silence from a beloved can make a loud
sound,
I ask myself why silence makes the greatest noise.

Humanity is the greatest Goliath
but falls prey to the David that is the earth.
I've often asked myself why ants can cause
so much pain to the greatest of animals.
Then it dawned upon me,
dynamites come in the smallest of packages.
Silence is not a weakness but a strength,
small isn't a disadvantage but an opportunity for
growth.

RIDING A BICYCLE

The spark of divine bliss does not let man
collapse in the throes of disappointment.
Man lives through chances and possibilities
that knows no end.
The end of one opportunity gives birth
to another opportunity.
Hence no scope for dejection.
that provisions were exhausted
and the time come to take shelter in silent obscurity.

DREAMS

As I close my eyes I sow the sky
like a fierce eagle.
Mounting up the hills I sing songs
of joy with everlasting laughter.
For I know when I close my eyes

I venture into a world of possibilities.
Dreams are the wings that carry me through
the rough storms of the dessert
and fuel my will like a burning furnace.
For when I close my eyes I become the
lava that melts all barricades that obscure my path.
To dream is to live
for if I was to restrain myself from dreaming
my soul would seize to exist .
And like a featherless eagle, I would toil
the earth waiting for my eyes to close
forever and free me from this burdensome world.

LOVE

Love is a choice
love is freedom, it is but the will
to wake up and choose the same person
all over again.
To jump from the sky and fall
knowing you have someone to pick you up.

To love is to learn to let go
to live in forever and know
tomorrow is not guaranteed.
Love is the wings that carry us through
difficult times.

Love is but a painful memory that we hold onto
and smile like the pain is appeasing to the soul.
To love is to swim across the devastating
frozen sea but feel the heat
of an erupting volcano.

Love is a choice
that comes without conditions
but promises of the fulfillment of self and one another.
For when you choose to love someone
you have mastered loving yourself.

PRISON

What is life but a prison
and pain but the defaults of oneself.
What is hatred but the need to belong
or death but the need to be loved.
To live is to escape the prison
one created by one in mind.
For it is when one carelessly seeks
to find themself that they are truly lost.

THE EYES TELL A STORY

Gazing upon your eyes
is to graze upon death's stare
Confronted with the pain
engraved within the eyes,
a soul yearning to be set free.
The eyes tell a story
of a condemned soul.
Pain and suffering are the residents
whose presence makes joy prisoner
sentenced behind the unescapable cell of the eyes.

I WISH I KNEW

As pressure pursued my patience,
curiosity came on with efficiency.
The passion for pleasure I couldn't measure,
consumed my innocence.
Like ripe fruit, I wanted to break open

but I was hardly a shoot,
Deceived by the pleasures
I thought I could conquer the world
but little did I know.

Like the desperate need to breathe
so became a man of any kind and in
a flash another life was clinging to mine.
The sudden snap of reality
caused a waterfall of cascading emotions
of regret.
Life had taken a drastic turn
leaving a shadow that I can never erase is then
that I wished I knew before causing decay to
my youthful nature.

CHARMED

Indulged in childlike laughter
He played me like my zodiac sign
changed the course of my horoscope.
A wolf in sheep's clothing,
he led me into the horrors of the woods
but I still thought it was haven

Euphoric love,
but when a dose of reality hit me
My life was already in shackles.
Sweet words just like the river Gangaa
making me feel like I was the chorus to my story
He lures me with his charm
but leaves me to drown in my tears
Like puffballs of the dandelion,
he vanished and his fiery love dimed.
My dreams have become distorted
Hopes mutilated
Society's myopic views before upon me.
My passion now lies in the mud
I became a stigmatization of the colony
I have become a vagabond in my nightmares
Inner monologuing the way he coaxed me,
rendering me helpless.
With just a gentle touch
my defenses came crashing down,
rumors of being charmed or coerced filled the sky
but failed to invade my love castle.
Reality earned a curious expression
as I first discovered the thorns in roses
that prickle the skin and damage the soul.

LOST LOVER

I was alone but you made me a crown,
You told me I was a queen on my own thrown
flabbergasted by your words I made you my own.

A heart's appeal fueled by a silky tongue
soft yet rigid.
Together we rode the wave of joy
and evoked a tsunami of happiness,
love like no other.

Today I sit alone
with death's cold embrace
hovering over my head,
the guilt of survival.
A beacon of emotional
triggered by losing you left me bereaved.

No one warned me about losing you
would cause my heart to come
to a standstill.
That love with all its strength.
is not immune to death.
Solely l have lost my path.
My heart is a fertile ground for wrath.

THE WEAKNESS IN ME

A ruined man fell from
her hand like a ripe fruit
to lie rotting on the ground.
In his demise, he became an adonis
His beauty makes the sun shy away
he is a magnet that drives my soul.

To fight against the feeling is futile
for I've fallen prey to your
dazzling godly beauty.
As I stare deep into his brown eyes
I become hypnotized.
I am enchanted by your words
my heart has become a loyal servant to you

Made in the USA
Columbia, SC
08 January 2023